YES TO HEALTH!
NO TO DRUGS!

Guidance about alcohol and drugs
for Primary School Children

By Alice McLoughlin

Illustrated by Mirona Mara

Copyright © 2017 by Alice McLoughlin

All rights reserved. No part of this publication may be reproduced in any form or by any means - graphic, electronic, or mechanical, including photocopying, recording, taping, or information storage and retrieval systems - without the prior written permission of the author.

All rights reserved.
ISBN: 1976092493
ISBN-13: 978-1976092497

To my mother

Bridget Hamilton O'Neill

INTRODUCTION

I have worked as a counsellor all my life, and one of my greatest areas of expertise is in helping people of all ages with alcohol and drug related problems. My experience of alcoholism and addiction began when I was 18 years old and studying psychology in Pennsylvania, USA. I volunteered every Saturday of First Year at Malvern Institute Treatment Centre, which was a half hour walk from Immaculata University. It would take another book to acknowledge everyone who has been part of my life journey in this work! I worked in the Aiseiri Treatment Centres in Cahir and Wexford, Ireland, for a total of eleven years, before setting up my private practice, which is on-going. I am deeply grateful for all of the learning, the challenges, the successes, and even the failures along the way, as they are part of a rich tapestry of my very interesting adventure.

For twenty years, I was invited to St. Joseph's Primary School in New Ross, County Wexford, (now part of Edmund Rice School) to speak with the sixth class students about the dangers of drugs and alcohol and the great benefits of avoiding drug use and of waiting until at least eighteen years of age to begin drinking. Using easily available information from many sources, along with my own insights, I developed a programme for transmitting what I think are the most urgent messages about drug and alcohol use, and I adapted and updated these messages over the years. Out of that programme came the idea to write a book for primary school children to convey in simple terms the dangers of alcohol and drug abuse and the attitudes and behaviours which will protect children from taking risks. As I spoke with hundreds of children over the years, I always felt that if this message could save even one child from the devastating effects of addiction, then it was indeed worthwhile. I offer this children's book in the same spirit of care and protection for our future generations.

Alice McLoughlin

Hello Boys and Girls…

As you grow up, there are so many things to learn about life. A very important lesson is to know which activities are good for your body and mind and which activities are harmful. This book will teach you about the dangers of alcohol and drugs.

What is a drug?

A drug is any substance which effects how a person thinks, feels, or behaves. A drug comes in many forms such as a tablet, a powder, a liquid, or a plant. Alcohol is a drug in liquid form. Because drugs change a person's mood, they can also be called mood altering substances. Drugs can be taken by drinking, smoking, sniffing, swallowing, or injecting.

Many drugs are legal, which means they are made with set ingredients in carefully controlled factories. These drugs are mostly sold in pharmacies and can be given by a doctor to help many illnesses. Examples of legal drugs are: painkillers, antibiotics, and antidepressants. Alcohol and nicotine in cigarettes are also legal drugs.

Many other drugs are illegal, which means that anyone who uses them is breaking the law and could go to prison. People who make illegal drugs do not care about the people who use the drugs. They only want to make lots of money for themselves. People selling such drugs often have addiction problems and can have very low levels of hygiene and handle the drugs with dirty hands and sneeze and cough on them, thus transmitting all kinds of germs to the user. Examples of illegal drugs are Marijuana, Ecstasy, Heroin, and Cocaine. Drugs can be attractive, especially some of the pills, which are colourful and look like fruity sweets and can tempt a person to try them.

All drugs are dangerous, but the illegal drugs are the most dangerous, because the people who make them use a variety of ingredients, and the person taking them has no idea exactly what they contain. Because they vary greatly in strength, illegal drugs can kill a person the very first time that a person uses them. Every year in Ireland, many people die from using illegal drugs.

With the help of an adult, make a list of legal and illegal drugs

Legal Drugs	Illegal Drugs
_____	_____
_____	_____
_____	_____
_____	_____

Alcohol

Alcohol is a sedative drug, a depressant, which means that it gradually puts the brain to sleep and causes the drinker to become drowsy and to have difficulty walking and talking. Alcohol is the most commonly used drug in Ireland and causes more problems than any other drug.

A young person whose body and mind is still developing is more affected by alcohol and other drugs than is an adult. Alcohol is distributed in bodily fluids, and boys have more fluid and less fat in their bodies than girls, so when a similar age boy and girl drink the same amount of alcohol, the girl will be more drunk than the boy. Girls therefore need to be extra aware of how alcohol is affecting them and make wise choices.

Beer contains less alcohol than wine or spirits such as whiskey or vodka or gin.

For example: Beer contains about 4-6 percent alcohol
               Wine contains about 12 percent
               Spirits contain about 40 percent

Healthy Ways to Drink Alcohol

As an adult, occasional drinking can be a pleasant social activity. It is always best to drink with others as drinking alone can lead to problems. Drinking should be part of another activity such as a meal or celebration. You will handle alcohol better if you drink slowly with food in your stomach. Eating food slows down the effects of alcohol.

If you choose to drink alcohol, always aim to be a social drinker who drinks moderately and has only one or two or three drinks on any occasion. At long events such as weddings, it can be helpful to drink a glass of water or a mineral in between the alcoholic drinks. It is good to have long periods where no alcohol is consumed as this gives the body, particularly the liver, time to rest from the effects of alcohol.

The Irish Culture of Drinking

Traditionally, Ireland has been a country in which many people drank heavily, and you may have witnessed people drinking in a way which is not healthy. In Ireland, it is common for people to drink up to 8 pints of beer in an evening. Just think about how you would feel if you drank 8 pints of water or 8 pints of coca cola! Eight pints is like a small bucket full of beer, and is never an appropriate amount to drink. In other countries such as Italy, France, Greece, and Portugal, people drink much smaller amounts and have fewer problems with alcohol.

Because the Irish drank heavily in the past, people from other countries think that all Irish people are the same and make jokes about the drunken Irish. When young Irish people go on holidays abroad, they often drink too much, and sometimes Irish emigrants in England, USA and Australia get involved in street rows and stabbings when drunk, and this has caused us to have a bad reputation in these places. Irish people cannot feel proud about their behaviour when drinking.

You are part of a new generation of Irish people, and, by making wise choices to drink only small amounts of alcohol, you can help to create a new image of Ireland. When you travel abroad, you are always representing your country, and Ireland is a wonderful country with beautiful scenery, friendly people, amazing music, and a rich history. If you decide to drink when you travel, always take only small amounts of alcohol, so that you will behave in a way that makes you feel good about yourself and that shows you are proud to be Irish.

Growing Up

There are many challenges to face as you go from childhood into your teenage years. Your body changes in many ways that feel strange for a while until you adjust to becoming an adult. You will have new feelings that may be exciting but also a bit scary. Sometimes you may worry about things, and it is important to have the courage to speak with an adult such as a parent, teacher, or older brother or sister about your concerns. Remember that every adult has also gone through adolescence, so they understand your feelings better than you may expect.

One of the challenges of adolescence is to learn how to be yourself and say how you really feel. You might feel pressure from your parents to be who they want you to be, and you might also feel pressure from your peers to be exactly like they are. You are a unique human being, no one else is exactly like you, and it is important to have the courage to express your own thoughts and opinions. It is also good to express yourself by choosing the clothes you like to wear, your hairstyle, and your activities. Pretending to be a person you are not will ultimately make you feel unhappy. Real friends will like you for being yourself. The more you express how you really feel, the more confident you will become.

When young people use alcohol or drugs to help them feel better and to boost their confidence, they actually stop themselves from learning good social skills, such as how to mix in a new group, how to speak with a stranger, or how to deal with making mistakes and saying sorry. By facing all these types of situations without relying on artificial support from alcohol or drugs, an adolescent becomes comfortable and grows in confidence. Everyone feels awkward and insecure at times, and the more you let yourself feel these feelings, the more you realise that the feelings always pass. Feelings are just part of being a human being.

It is so important to really live through and experience the ups and downs of your teenage years. Remember you will never get this time back. So don't rush ahead. Learn all you can about being a teenager. If you make a mistake, just learn from that mistake and move on. Do your best to be kind to yourself and to other people who also want to be accepted! Be grateful for all the interesting experiences of being a teenager. Once you become an adult, you will have many years to experience all the things that are part of adult life.

So enjoy every day of NOW!

Reasons why young people drink and use drugs

1. Curiosity. Young people may desire to know what drinking or taking drugs feels like. It is good to wait until the legal age of 18 or older to try alcohol, and it is very wise to decide never to take illegal drugs as they are very dangerous and can cause injury and even death the very first time you take them.

2. Influence of Friends. It is best to spend time with friends who make healthy choices to avoid alcohol and drugs. If you are in a group of people who are drinking or trying a drug, it is ok to say "No." Anybody who makes you feel bad by putting pressure on you is not a real friend, so avoid spending time with people like that. If you are very uncomfortable at a party or social event because of the way others are behaving, it might be wise to phone an adult to take you home. Your safety is always the most important thing.

3. To feel Grown Up. It is important to enjoy every moment when you are young. It is more mature to make choices to avoid alcohol until 18 and to decide never to take drugs than it is to risk your health and your life. The body and mind of a young person are still developing and are more easily damaged by alcohol and drugs than are the body and mind of a fully-grown adult.

4. Rebellion against Parents. Being a teenager is about becoming more independent and making more choices about your life. It is understandable that you will not always agree with your parents, and it is good to express your feelings and come to an agreement. Alcohol and drugs are unhealthy choices, and, if you use alcohol and drugs to rebel against your parents, you are seriously hurting yourself as well as them. Good choices are to experiment with decorating your room, wearing interesting clothes, choosing your favourite music, or trying fun hairstyles.

5. Desire for Pleasure. You can have lots of fun in healthy ways by spending time with friends, listening to or playing music, chatting, playing sports, or engaging in any hobby that you enjoy. The pleasure given by alcohol and other drugs is very temporary and wears off quickly, whereas the joy of doing fun activities with friends and family will create good feelings that last for a long time in your mind.

6. Imitating Bad Habits of Family Members. Some families have a culture of drinking or drug use and may have addiction in several generations of the family. If you live in such a family, there can be huge pressure to start drinking or taking drugs. It can seem like the normal thing to do, and it can feel very difficult to make different choices, but it is not impossible. If your parents have problems themselves and are unable to support your healthy choices, you might need to turn to a trusted adult outside the family such as a teacher, school counsellor, or sports instructor.

7. Exam pressure. Secondary School exams, particularly the Leaving Certificate, can cause a lot of stress. It is important to put these exams in perspective. Even if a student does not perform well, there are many interesting courses and jobs which do not demand high grades. Many successful people never passed an exam. Using alcohol and drugs lessens concentration and memory and therefore is never helpful. Exercise and deep breathing are healthy choices to reduce exam stress.

6. To Cope with Painful Feelings. Insecurity, loneliness, depression, or any other painful emotions are a normal part of life just like the positive emotions of happiness, gratitude, and love. All feelings change and pass. When you experience negative emotions, it will help if you tell someone exactly how you feel and ask for support until you feel better. It also helps to do something to distract yourself such as exercise or music. You will become stronger and more confident by coping with the emotions rather than avoiding them with alcohol and drugs.

Consequences of Drinking and Drug Taking for Young People

1. Lowered motivation at school. Because alcohol and other drugs affect the mind, young people can have poorer concentration and memory and may perform less well in exams. In addition, energy levels will be lower for a day or two after drinking or using drugs, and so school work will suffer.

2. Fights and Injuries. Every year in Ireland, many people die from injuries received during alcohol and drug induced aggression. Stabbing has become common during fights among drunken young people.

3. Road accidents. Driving is always impaired by drink and drugs, and people who walk on the roads while under the influence are also at a risk of stumbling under a passing car. It is a big mistake to think that taking a cold shower or drinking coffee will make a person sober enough to drive. The fact is that it takes several hours for the body to break down alcohol or drugs and for the mind to be clear enough to drive.

4. Drowning. Up to a third of deaths from drowning in Ireland are alcohol-related. A person should never swim when under the influence of alcohol or drugs.

5. Risk of Death from the Direct Effects of Alcohol and Drugs. Counsellors frequently help the families and friends of people who have died from alcohol and drug abuse. One example is a fifteen year old girl who collapsed after drinking vodka, vomited, and smothered as a result of the vomit going into her lungs because she was lying on her back and unable to swallow. Another example is a drunken man who got a lift home from the pub, stepped out of the car, stumbled and fell backwards, hitting the back of his head on the ground causing serious brain injury and death. Such deaths leave family and friends feeling broken-hearted.

6. Suicide. Everyone has upset feelings, and sometimes you can feel very sad, lonely, depressed. These feelings will ALWAYS pass, and telling someone about them or doing an activity such as exercise or listening to music will help the painful feelings to pass more quickly. When a person takes alcohol or drugs, the painful feelings are heightened, and he/she is more likely to think about death and to do something impulsive which may lead to death. This causes a lifetime of pain for the family and friends of the person.

7. Crime. Alcohol and drugs are expensive and can cause young people to become involved in theft to obtain money to buy them. In addition, because people take more risks when drinking and behave impulsively, drinkers can damage property or get involved with the law just by being drunk and noisy. If a young person gets into trouble with the law because of drug use, he/she may never be allowed into countries such as the USA and Australia.

8. Psychological Dependence. This means that when a person has an uncomfortable mood or frame of mind, he or she depends on alcohol or drugs to change it. Eventually he/she needs alcohol or drugs just to do normal things such as talk to new people or ask someone out on a date. The person is depending on alcohol or drugs for confidence and good feelings, and gradually life becomes more and more focused on getting the alcohol and drugs and neglecting other activities. It is important for teenagers to learn to have fun and find pleasure in a range of activities such as sports, exercise, chatting with friends, art, reading, cinema, music, etc. Drug induced pleasure lasts very briefly and creates many problems, whereas pleasure from healthy activities builds a happy life.

9. Bad treatment from Other People. When a person is under the influence of alcohol or drugs, other people can take advantage and may rob or injure the person. Occasionally, someone may spike a drink by secretly dropping a drug into it, which causes the drinker to become drowsy or unconscious and unable to remember, and allows horrible things to happen. It is wise therefore to not accept drink from strangers and to always keep your glass in your hand.

10. Difficulties Related to Sex. Because drugs and alcohol make people feel braver, young people sometimes have unprotected sex with a stranger and can risk getting a sexual disease, and girls risk becoming pregnant. Sex can be a very special act between two grown-up people who know and care about one another, but when young people who are drugged or drunk have sex with a stranger, it often makes them feel ashamed and can lead to low self-esteem.

Avoid danger now, and you will have a bright future!

In an Emergency

Hopefully you will never witness an emergency caused by alcohol or drugs, but if you are ever in the company of a person who takes too much and who gets very drowsy or unconscious, here are some guidelines about what to do:

1. **Never leave the person alone,** *but speak to them and comfort and reassure them.*
2. **Do not give them anything to eat or drink** *because they may not be able to swallow and could choke or smother.*
3. **Always turn them on to their side** *to prevent them inhaling vomit if they get sick.*
4. **Immediately phone for a doctor or ambulance.**
5. **If drugs have been taken, tell the ambulance crew** *what you think they might have taken and give any substance or implement they used in drug taking to the doctor or ambulance crew.*

Alcoholism and Addiction

Because alcohol and drugs affect the brain and numb unwanted feelings, it is easy to become addicted to these substances. Addiction means that a person needs to drink or use drugs even though they cause a long list of very serious problems to physical and mental health, to the family, to friendships, to work, and to finances. Some young people mistakenly believe that marijuana, which is known by many other names such as grass, cannabis, weed, or hash, is a soft drug and not addictive, but that is absolutely not true. All drugs including alcohol and hash are addictive and cause serious problems when used regularly. Using cannabis greatly increases the chances of developing mental health problems in the future. Addiction hurts the person who becomes dependent on alcohol and drugs, and it is also devastating to family and to everyone close to the addicted person.

Alcoholism and addiction can happen to anyone no matter what type of home you come from or how educated you are. Studies show that if you have a parent who is addicted, you yourself are more likely to become addicted, and therefore you need to be always careful about alcohol use by not drinking at all or drinking only small amounts.

More and more young people are developing problems with alcohol. In the U.S.A., numerous studies indicate that people who begin drinking or using drugs in the teens are more likely to progress into addiction. One study from the National Institute on Alcohol Abuse and Alcoholism studied 43,000 people and found that young people who began drinking before Age 15 were four times more likely to develop alcoholism than those who began at age 21. The findings were as follows:

Began drinking under age 15…….40% develop alcoholism

Began drinking at age 17…………..24.5% develop alcoholism

Began drinking after age 21……….10% develop alcoholism

This means that it is wise for you to wait as long as possible before you start to drink. Every year you wait will give you time to develop physically, mentally, and emotionally. This time improves your chances of not developing an addiction. Irish law recommends that you wait until at least 18 to try alcohol, but waiting until 21 is even better. Real friends will always respect your right to say "No" to alcohol and will not put pressure on you to drink even if they choose to do so. You have a right to make your own choices, and your confidence will grow when you do so.

Asking for Help

At any time, if you are worried about your own use of alcohol or drugs or about someone else, a lot of help is available. The first step is to have the courage to tell an adult you really trust such as a parent, grandparent, other relative, or a teacher or friend. A local doctor will usually know about the types of help available in your area and how to contact them. Abuse of alcohol and drugs makes people sick, but with the correct help many people succeed in giving up the addiction and can recover and live very fulfilling and happy lives.

Types of help include counselling, self-help groups, and residential treatment. Talking with a counsellor helps the addicted person to understand the problems caused by the addiction and to make healthy choices about giving up the alcohol or drugs. Self-help groups such as Alcoholics Anonymous AA or Narcotics Anonymous NA offer the support of other people who are also doing their best to recover from an addiction. Residential treatment is like a hospital where a person with a drug or alcohol problem can live for a few weeks and receive counselling and support to get back to a healthy way of living. When people with addictions have counselling and the backing of others with whom to share their worries and concerns, they are less likely to use alcohol and drugs and have a better chance of recovery.

Your Inner Light

Each person is unique and special. There is no one else in the whole world exactly like you, and no one else can do what you came to do in this world. You have your own inner light. You can talk to this light and ask it for help, strength, and guidance at any time. It is always inside of you and, just like putting wind to a fire, your inner light will get bigger and brighter every time you talk to it and give it attention. The world needs people with bright inner light, and when your own light is strong, you help to brighten other people's days.

Some activities increase your inner light, and some activities decrease your inner light. Being around people who make you feel bad or upset dims your own light. Using drugs and alcohol are also examples of activities which decrease your inner light. Other activities which lessen your inner light are eating a lot of foods with artificial ingredients, spending too much time on electronic devices such as phones, pads, and laptops and watching violent films or games. It is therefore wise to spend only small amounts of time on these activities.

Many positive fun activities add to your inner light and help you to shine more brightly. Examples of uplifting activities are walking in nature, such as on a beach, in a forest, or up a mountain. Being out in the fresh air and daylight are always helpful, as are all forms of exercise. Other activities which increase your inner light are music, art, and dancing. Eating good natural foods such as fruit and vegetables brightens your light, as does being around people who make you feel happy and loved. So it is best to choose lots of these pursuits.

Keeping your inner light strong will make it easier for you to cope with all the ups and downs that are part of life. It is a good idea to ask for help from your inner light every day. That light will protect you and make you feel confident. When your inner light is strong, you will not need to use alcohol or drugs, and your life will be happier.

Summary

All drugs are dangerous, and alcohol is a dangerous drug. It is good to protect your precious body and mind by refusing to take illegal drugs and by waiting until you are at least 18 before taking alcohol. Good friends will always like you, even when you say no to drugs and alcohol. People who put pressure on you to do anything which is uncomfortable for you are not real friends and are best avoided. Always talk to an adult you trust when you are worried about anything.

Most of all, be aware of the bright light within yourself, and think about it, and ask it for help many times every day of your life.

May your life be blessed with everything that is good and healthy!

To order copies of this book, please contact the author, **Alice McLoughlin**, by visiting **www.alicemcloughlin.com**